# Introduction

There are times when you want and need a fast and easy quilt pattern. Sometimes all you have is an afternoon free here and there to devote to your craft. And, of course, there are times when you really want to make a very special gift, but you don't have a lot of time to dedicate to making it. Well, being short on time won't stop you from making that special quilt when you have *Jiffy Quick Quilts* at your disposal. This book will allow you to make the most out of your available time.

*Jiffy Quick Quilts* has eight quilts, all with size options, plus a bed runner and a table runner. The patterns were designed for both speed and versatility. Your fabric choices and these excellent patterns will give you endless possibilities. You can make everything from baby quilts to quilts that are perfect for the "man cave." It's all here—the designs and the instructions. All you need to do is add fabric and get stitching.

*Jiffy Quick Quilts* is destined to be your go-to book for both patterns and inspiration.

# Table of Contents

# Cake Walk

This quilt uses precut 10" squares or enough fabric to cut your own. Either way, here is a fast and easy project.

Design by Nancy Scott
Quilted by Masterpiece Quilting

## Skill Level
Beginner

## Specifications
Quilt Size: 62" x 72"

## Materials
- 19 assorted precut 10" A squares
- ⅝ yard binding fabric
- 2¾ yards aqua dot
- Backing to size
- Batting to size
- Thread
- Basic sewing tools and supplies

## Project Notes
Read all instructions before beginning this project.

Stitch right sides together using a ¼" seam allowance unless otherwise specified.

Materials and cutting lists assume 40" of usable fabric width.

## Designer Tip

*Use as many different precut squares as you like, or use duplicate fabrics as shown in the sample quilt.*

## Cutting

### From 6 precut 10" A squares:
- Subcut squares in half across width to make 12 (5" x 10") B rectangles.

### From binding fabric:
- Cut 7 (2½" by fabric width) strips for binding.

### From aqua dot:
- Cut 2 (10" by fabric width) strips.
  Subcut strips into 20 (3½" x 10") C rectangles.
- Cut 1 (3" by fabric width) strip.
  Subcut strip into 4 (3" x 10") D rectangles.
- Cut 6 (3½" by fabric width) E strips.
- Cut 7 (6½" by fabric width) F/G strips.

## Completing the Quilt
Refer to the Assembly Diagram on page 4 for positioning of rows and strips for steps 3–6.

**1.** Join three A squares, two B rectangles and four C rectangles as shown in Figure 1; press. Repeat to make three of row 1.

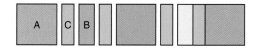

**Figure 1**

**2.** Join two D rectangles, two A squares, three B rectangles and four C rectangles as shown in Figure 2; press. Repeat to make two of row 2.

**Figure 2**

**3.** Join the E strips on the short ends to make a long strip; press. Subcut strip into four 3½" x 50" E sashing strips.

**4.** Join the rows alternating with E sashing strips to complete the quilt center; press.

**5.** Join the F/G strips on the short ends to make a long strip; press. Subcut strip into two 6½" x 60" F strips and two 6½" x 62" G strips.

**6.** Sew F strips to opposite sides of the quilt center and G strips to the top and bottom to complete the quilt top; press.

**7.** Create a quilt sandwich referring to Quilting Basics on page 44.

**8.** Quilt as desired.

**9.** Bind referring to Quilting Basics on page 44 to finish. ●

## Inspiration

*"I love fabrics with medium- to large-size prints, and Cake Walk is perfect for showcasing such beautiful fabrics."* —Nancy Scott

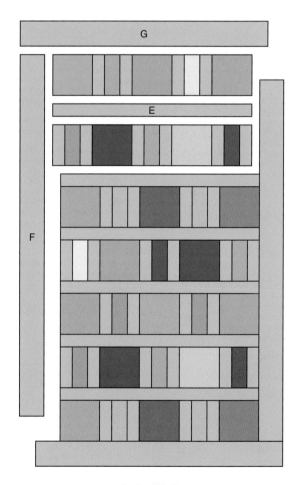

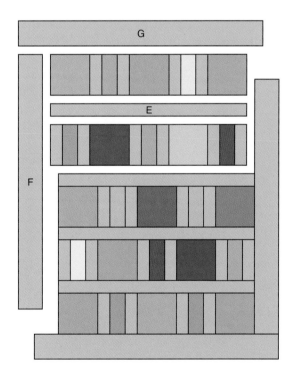

**Cake Walk**
Assembly Diagram 62" x 72"

**Cake Walk**
Alternate-Size Assembly Diagram 62" x 82"
Add 2 rows & 2 sashing strips
to make a twin-size quilt.

# Lemonade

Three fabrics and a free weekend and you
can have this top ready to quilt.

Designed & Quilted by Denise Russell

## Skill Level
Confident Beginner

## Specifications
Quilt Size: 45" x 63"
Block Size: 9" x 9" finished
Number of Blocks: 35

## Materials
- 1⅜ yards gray with white dots
- 1½ yards yellow print
- 1½ yards white solid
- Backing to size
- Batting to size
- Thread
- Basic sewing tools and supplies

## Project Notes
Read all instructions before beginning this project.

Stitch right sides together using a ¼" seam allowance unless otherwise specified.

Materials and cutting lists assume 40" of usable fabric width.

## Cutting

### From gray with white dots:
- Cut 7 (3¾" by fabric width) strips.
  Subcut strips into 70 (3¾") B squares.
- Cut 6 (2½" by fabric width) strips for binding.

### From yellow print:
- Cut 9 (5" by fabric width) strips.
  Subcut strips into 70 (5") A squares.

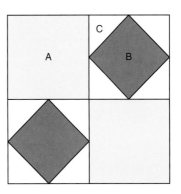

**Lemonade Four-Patch**
9" x 9" Finished Block
Make 35

### From white solid:
- Cut 13 (3¼" by fabric width) strips.
  Subcut strips into 140 (3¼") C squares. Cut each
  C square in half on 1 diagonal to make 280
  C triangles.

## Completing the Blocks
**1.** Fold a B square in half both directions and finger-press to make a crease to mark the center. With wrong sides together, fold four C triangles in half and crease to mark the center.

**2.** Referring to Figure 1a, lay two C triangles on opposite sides of the B square, right sides together, so the creases match up. Sew triangles to the square; press open (Figure 1b). In the same manner, add remaining C triangles to the remaining sides of the B square as shown in Figure 1c. Press and trim units to measure 5" square if necessary.

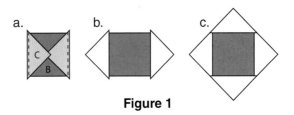

**Figure 1**

**3.** Repeat steps 1 and 2 to make 70 B-C units.

**4.** Stitch an A square to a B-C unit to make a row. Repeat to make two rows. Stitch rows together as shown in Figure 2. Repeat to make 35 blocks.

Make 35

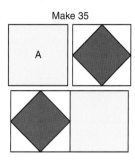

**Figure 2**

## Designer Tip

*For quick construction, chain-piece white triangles to gray squares. Then, chain-piece gray/white squares to yellow squares, and finally, do the same to form each block.*

## Completing the Quilt

Refer to the Assembly Diagram for positioning of blocks and rows for steps 1 and 2.

**1.** Join five blocks to make a row, rotating blocks to form pattern as shown; press. Repeat to make a total of seven rows.

**2.** Join the rows to complete the quilt center; press.

**3.** Create a quilt sandwich referring to Quilting Basics on page 44.

**4.** Quilt as desired.

**5.** Bind referring to Quilting Basics on page 44 to finish. ●

**Lemonade**
Alternate-Size Assembly Diagram 54" x 90"
Add 1 block to each row & 3 rows to
the length to make a twin-size quilt.

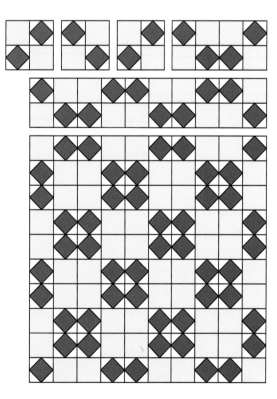

**Lemonade**
Assembly Diagram 45" x 63"

# Inspiration

*"Pitchers with lemonade and tumblers on a picnic table in a summer afternoon as children run around the sunny backyard inspired me to create this bright and cheerful quilt."* —Denise Russell

# Fly Right

This bed runner is easier than it looks. Just two fabrics and a bit of folding create the 3-D diamond at the intersection of the squares. You'll be done in a jiffy!

Design by Gina Gempesaw
Quilted by Carole Whaling

## Skill Level
Confident Beginner

## Specifications
Runner Size: 70" x 28"
Block Size: 14" x 14" finished
Number of Blocks: 10

## Materials
- ½ yard binding fabric
- ⅝ yard red tonal
- 1 yard large print
- 1 yard black dot
- Backing to size
- Batting to size
- Thread
- Basic sewing tools and supplies

## Project Notes
Read all instructions before beginning this project.

Stitch right sides together using a ¼" seam allowance unless otherwise specified.

Materials and cutting lists assume 40" of usable fabric width.

## Cutting

### From binding fabric:
- Cut 6 (2¼" by fabric width) strips.

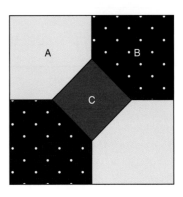

**Bow Tie**
14" x 14" Finished Block
Make 10

### From red tonal:
- Cut 3 (6" by fabric width) strips.
    Subcut strips into 14 (6") C squares.

### From large print:
- Cut 4 (7½" by fabric width) strips.
    Subcut strips into 20 (7½") A squares.

### From black dot:
- Cut 4 (7½" by fabric width) strips.
    Subcut strips into 20 (7½") B squares.

## Completing the Runner
Refer to the Placement Diagram for positioning of blocks and pieces for steps 1–3.

**1.** Referring to the 3-D Bow-Tie Technique sidebar and block drawing, make 10 Bow Tie blocks.

**2.** Lay out the 10 Bow Tie blocks in two rows of 5 blocks each.

**3.** Join the blocks into rows and the rows into the runner using the remaining C squares and following the 3-D Bow Ties sidebar.

**4.** Create a quilt sandwich referring to Quilting Basics on page 44.

**5.** Quilt as desired.

**6.** Bind referring to Quilting Basics on page 44 to finish. ●

## Inspiration

*"The classic Bow Tie block inspired this quilt."* —Gina Gempesaw

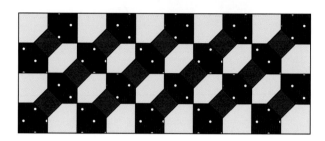

**Fly Right**
Placement Diagram 70" x 28"

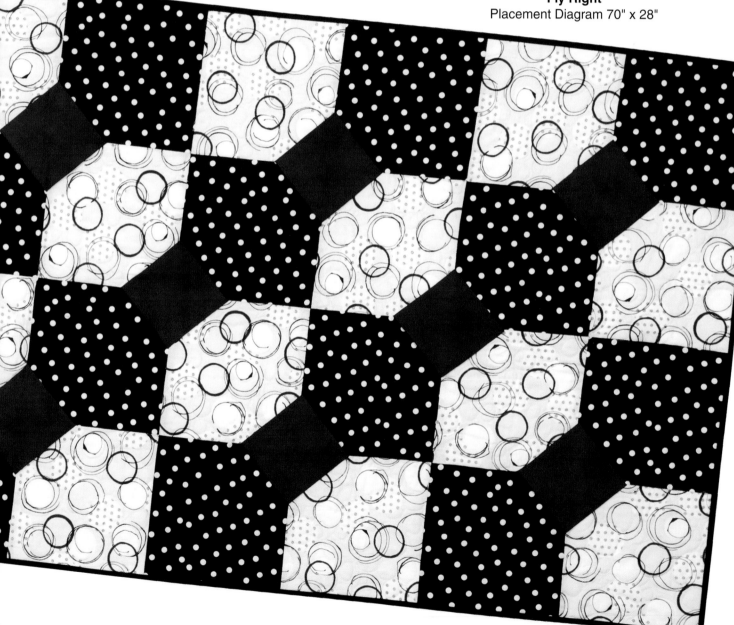

# 3-D Bow-Tie Technique

Careful folding and stitching adds a 3-D element to these easy blocks. Simply follow the steps below!

**1.** Fold one C square in half with wrong sides together to make a 3" x 6" rectangle. Do not press.

**2.** Sandwich the folded C square between one A and one B square, right sides together, and matching top and right-hand side raw edges; stitch together along the right edge referring to Figure A.

**Figure A**

**3.** Open the stitched unit and fold the A and B squares away from the folded C rectangle as shown in Figure B

**Figure B**

**4.** Place the short unstitched edge of the folded C square between a second pair of A and B squares, alternating the positioning of the squares from the opposite ends as shown in Figure C.

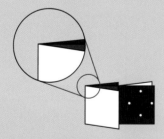

**Figure C**

**5.** Stitch and open the unit as in steps 2 and 3, referring to Figure D.

**Figure D**

**6.** Open the folded C pocket and spread apart with your fingers, pulling the A and B squares together; match the seams and align the raw edges of the C pocket with the edges of the A-B unit referring to Figure E.

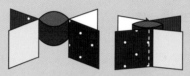

**Figure E**

**7.** Stitch across the long edge; open and press the seams in opposite directions and the C pocket flat to complete one Bow Tie block referring to Figure F and the block drawing.

**Figure F**

# Tiny Bubbles

### All you need to make this gorgeous quilt is some free time and a collection of pretty fat quarters.

Designed & Quilted by Julie Weaver

## Skill Level
Confident Beginner

## Specifications
Quilt Size: 48" x 58"
Block Size: 9" x 9" finished
Number of Blocks: 14

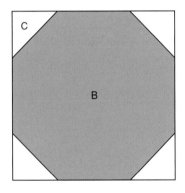

**Block 1**
9" x 9" Finished Block
Make 1

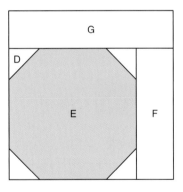

**Block 2**
9" x 9" Finished Block
Make 3

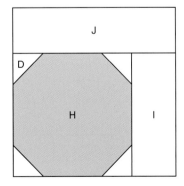

**Block 3**
9" x 9" Finished Block
Make 3

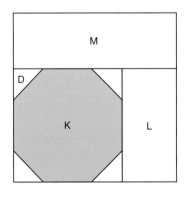

**Block 4**
9" x 9" Finished Block
Make 3

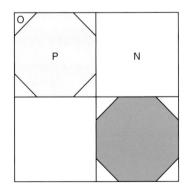

**Block 5**
9" x 9" Finished Block
Make 4

## Project Notes

Read all instructions before beginning this project.

Stitch right sides together using a ¼" seam allowance unless otherwise specified.

Materials and cutting lists assume 40" of usable fabric width.

## Cutting

### From variety of 14 fat quarters:

- Cut 1 (9½") B square.
- Cut 3 (7½") E squares.
- Cut 3 (7") H squares.
- Cut 3 (6½") K squares.
- Cut 8 (5") P squares.

### From variety of all 18 fat quarters:

- Cut 32 (3½" x 5") T rectangles and 26 (3½" x 5½") U rectangles.
- Cut 4 (5" x 5½") S rectangles.

### From aqua print:

- Cut 5 (2" by fabric width) Q/R strips.
- Cut 6 (2¼" by fabric width) strips for binding.

### From white solid:

- Cut 2 (9½" by fabric width) strips.
  Subcut strips into 6 (9½") A squares.
- Cut 2 (2½" by fabric width) strips.
  Subcut strips into 3 (2½" x 7½") F rectangles,
    3 (2½" x 9½") G rectangles and 4 (2½")
    C squares.
- Cut 3 (2" by fabric width) strips.
  Subcut strips into 36 (2") D squares.
- Cut 2 (3" by fabric width) strips.
  Subcut strips into 3 (3" x 7") I rectangles and
    3 (3" x 9½") J rectangles.
- Cut 2 (3½" by fabric width) strips.
  Subcut strips into 3 (3½" x 6½") L rectangles
    and 3 (3½" x 9½") M rectangles.
- Cut 1 (5" by fabric width) strip.
  Subcut strip into 8 (5") N squares.
- Cut 2 (1½" by fabric width) strips.
  Subcut strips into 32 (1½") O squares.

**Designer Tip**

*Blocks 2, 3 and 4 in this quilt are quite similar. To achieve the design exactly as shown, pay close attention when arranging the blocks.*

## Completing the Blocks

**1.** Draw a diagonal line from corner to corner on the wrong side of each C, D and O square.

**2.** Referring to Figure 1, place a C square right sides together on one corner of the B square. Stitch on the drawn line and trim seam allowance to ¼". Press C to the right side. Repeat on remaining three corners to complete Block 1.

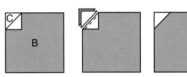

**Figure 1**

**3.** In the same manner, add D squares to all four corners of an E square. Referring to Figure 2, sew an F rectangle to the right side of the E-D unit. Add a G rectangle to the top edge to complete Block 2 referring to the block drawing. Repeat to make three Block 2 blocks.

**Figure 2**

**4.** Using four D squares, and one each H, I and J pieces, complete Block 3 referring to steps 2 and 3, and the block drawing. Repeat to make three Block 3 blocks.

**5.** Using four D squares, and one each K, L and M pieces, complete Block 4 referring to steps 2 and 3, and the block drawing. Repeat to make three Block 4 blocks.

**6.** Stitch O squares to all four corners of a P square referring to Figure 1 and step 2. Repeat to make eight O-P units.

**7.** Stitch an O-P unit to an N square to make a row. Repeat to make two rows. Stitch rows together as shown in Figure 3. Repeat steps 6 and 7 to make four Block 5 blocks.

**Figure 3**

## Completing the Quilt

Refer to the Assembly Diagram for positioning of blocks, strips and pieces for steps 1–5.

**1.** Lay out the Blocks 1–5 and six A squares into 5 rows of 4 blocks and squares each. Sew the blocks and squares into rows.

**2.** Join the rows to complete the quilt center; press.

**3.** Join the Q/R strips on the short ends to make a long strip; press. Subcut the strip into two each 2" x 45½" Q strips and 2" x 39½" R strips. Sew Q strips to opposite sides of the quilt center and R strips to the top and bottom; press.

**4.** Sew 16 T rectangles long sides together as shown in Figure 4 to make a side border strip. Repeat to make a second side border strip. Sew to opposite sides of the quilt top.

**Figure 4**

**5.** In the same manner and referring to Figure 5, sew 13 U rectangles long sides together to make a top/bottom border strip. Sew an S rectangle to each end of the U strip. Repeat to make a second top/bottom border strip. Sew to the top and bottom of the quilt top.

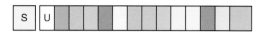

**Figure 5**

**6.** Create a quilt sandwich referring to Quilting Basics on page 44.

**7.** Quilt as desired.

**8.** Bind referring to Quilting Basics on page 44 to finish. ●

## Designer Tip

*It's easy to adjust the length of a pieced border simply by taking a little bigger or smaller seam when sewing the rectangles together.*

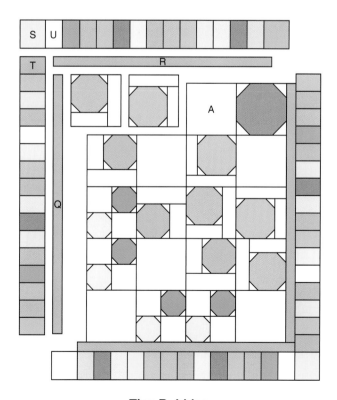

**Tiny Bubbles**
Assembly Diagram 48" x 58"

# Inspiration

*"The inspiration for this quilt, of course, was the initial challenge to design something that could be made in a jiffy. Lately I've been trying to design quilts that are a bit more contemporary in style. Fabric companies right now are producing such fun contemporary fabrics that need to be made into quilts! Although the fabric I chose isn't a contemporary style in my opinion, I think the quilt is. It's a start on my contemporary journey!" —Julie Weaver*

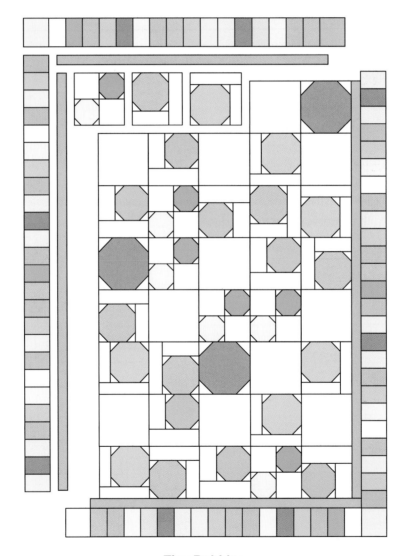

**Tiny Bubbles**
Alternate-Size Assembly Diagram 57" x 85"
Add 1 block to each row & 3 rows to
the length to make a twin-size quilt.

# Twist It & Turn It

Pick a fun focus fabric for the large squares and pull the colors out of it for the pieced block.

Design by Gina Gempesaw
Quilted by Carole Whaling

## Skill Level
Confident Beginner

## Specifications
Quilt Size: 50" x 70"
Block Size: 10" x 10" finished
Number of Blocks: 17

## Materials
- ¼ yard each 2 light gray tonals
- ¼ yard each 4 medium gray and red tonals
- ¼ yard black tonal
- ⅓ yard light red tonal
- ⅓ yard black check
- ½ yard each 4 light prints
- ⅝ yard binding fabric
- 2 yards large print
- Backing to size
- Batting to size
- Thread
- Basic sewing tools and supplies

## Project Notes
Read all instructions before beginning this project.

Stitch right sides together using a ¼" seam allowance unless otherwise specified.

Materials and cutting lists assume 40" of usable fabric width.

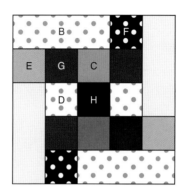

**Twist It & Turn It**
10" x 10" Finished Block
Make 17

## Cutting

### From light gray tonals:
- Cut 3 (2½" by fabric width) D strips.

### From medium gray and red tonals:
- Cut 6 (2½" by fabric width) G strips.

### From black tonal:
- Cut 2 (2½" by fabric width) H strips.

### From light red tonal:
- Cut 3 (2½" by fabric width) E strips.

### From black check:
- Cut 3 (2½" by fabric width) F strips.

### From 4 light prints:
- Cut 6 (6½" by fabric width) B strips.

### From 2 light prints:
- Cut 4 (2½" by fabric width) C strips.

**From binding fabric:**
- Cut 7 (2¼" by fabric width) strips.

**From large print:**
- Cut 6 (10½" by fabric width) strips. Subcut strips into 18 (10½") A squares.

## Completing the Blocks

**1.** Sew a B strip to an E strip along length to make a B-E strip set; press seam toward B. Repeat to make two more strip sets. Subcut strip sets into 34 (2½") B-E segments as shown in Figure 1.

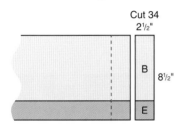

Cut 34
2½"

B  8½"

E

**Figure 1**

**2.** Repeat step 1 with F strips and remaining B strips to cut 34 (2½") B-F segments as shown in Figure 2.

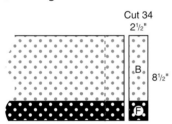

Cut 34
2½"

B  8½"

F

**Figure 2**

**3.** Referring to Figure 3, sew a G strip to opposite long sides of a D strip to make a D-G strip set; press seams toward G strips. Repeat to make two more strip sets. Subcut strip sets into 34 (2½") D-G segments.

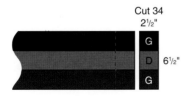

Cut 34
2½"

G
D  6½"
G

**Figure 3**

**4.** Referring to Figure 4, repeat step 3 with H strips and C strips to make two C-H strip sets; press seams toward H. Cut strip sets into 17 (2½") C-H segments.

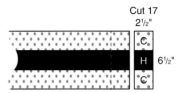

Cut 17
2½"

C
H  6½"
C

**Figure 4**

**5.** Referring to Figure 5, lay out D-G segments on both long sides of a C-H segment. Sew the segments together to make a nine-patch unit; press seams toward D-G segments. Repeat to make 17 units.

Make 17

G  C  G
D  H  D
G  C  G

**Figure 5**

**6.** Referring to the Partial Seams Construction sidebar on page 21 and the block drawing, add two each B-E and B-F segments to four sides of a nine-patch unit to complete the block. Repeat to make 17 blocks.

## Completing the Quilt

Refer to the Assembly Diagram on page 20 for positioning of blocks, squares and rows for steps 1 and 2.

**1.** Join two blocks alternating with three A squares to make row A; press. Repeat to make a total of four A rows. Join three blocks alternating with two A squares to make row B; press. Repeat to make a total of three B rows.

**2.** Join the A and B rows to complete the quilt top; press.

**3.** Create a quilt sandwich referring to Quilting Basics on page 44.

**4.** Quilt as desired.

**5.** Bind referring to Quilting Basics on page 44 to finish. ●

## Inspiration

*"Black and white graphic art inspired this quilt. Shades of gray and red soften the look."* —Gina Gempesaw

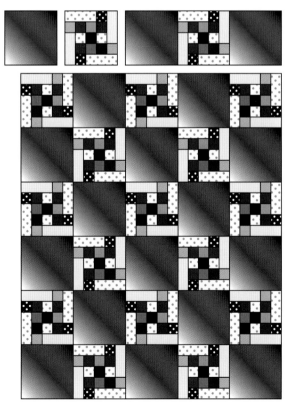

**Twist It & Turn It**
Assembly Diagram 50" x 70"

**Twist It & Turn It**
Alternate-Size Assembly Diagram 60" x 90"
Add 1 block to each row & 2 rows to
length to make a twin-size quilt.

# Partial Seam Construction

Create a seamless wraparound look for the Twist It & Turn It block using partial seams. Once you understand how to do it, this technique is easy!

**1.** Referring to Figure A, start sewing a B-E segment to the left side of a nine-patch unit. Stop 1" from the bottom of the nine-patch unit; press.

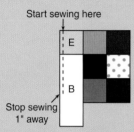

**Figure A**

**2.** Join a B-F segment to the top, sewing along the entire length from the outside edge toward the nine-patch unit referring to Figure B; press.

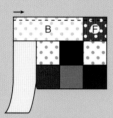

**Figure B**

**3.** Referring to Figure C, add a B-E segment to the right side in the same manner.

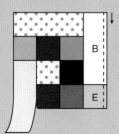

**Figure C**

**4.** Sew a B/F segment to the bottom in the same manner, referring to Figure D and making sure not to catch first B-E segment in stitching; press.

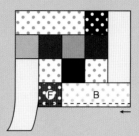

**Figure D**

**5.** Flip the first B/E segment onto the block, right sides together, and stitch from the stopping point in step 1 to the edge of the block as shown in Figure E; press.

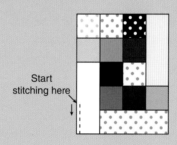

**Figure E**

# Building Blocks

There are lots of possibilities for this pattern. Go scrappy or pick a color scheme—just pair lights with darks to create the same type of look.

*Designed & Quilted by Julie Weaver*

## Skill Level
Beginner

## Specifications
Quilt Size: 52" x 62"
Block Size: 10" x 10" finished
Number of Blocks: 20

## Materials
- 5 fat quarters assorted pink prints
- 5 fat quarters assorted white prints
- ¾ yard white/pink floral
- 1¼ yards pink print
- Backing to size
- Batting to size
- Thread
- Basic sewing tools and supplies

## Project Notes
Read all instructions before beginning this project.

Stitch right sides together using a ¼" seam allowance unless otherwise specified.

Materials and cutting lists assume 40" of usable fabric width.

## Cutting

### From 3 pink & 2 white fat quarters:
- Cut 3 (6½" x 18") A strips from each.

### From 2 pink & 3 white fat quarters:
- Cut 3 (4½" x 18") B strips from each.

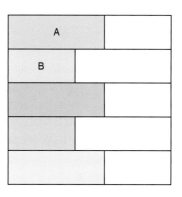

**Building Block**
10" x 10" Finished Block
Make 20

### From white/pink floral:
- Cut 6 (3½" by fabric width) E/F strips.

### From pink print:
- Cut 11 (2" by fabric width) C/D/G/H strips.
- Cut 6 (2¼" by fabric width) strips for binding.

## Completing the Blocks

**1.** Make three piles, each containing three matching pink A strips and three matching white B strips; number piles 1, 3 and 5. Make two piles, each containing two matching white A strips and two matching pink B strips; number piles 2 and 4.

**2.** From pile #1, select and sew a pink A strip to a white B strip along length to make a strip set; press. Repeat to make three strip sets. Referring to Figure 1, subcut strips into 20 (2½" x 10½") #1 units. Keep units in a separate pile or a labeled bag.

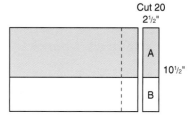

Cut 20
2½"

A

10½"

B

**Figure 1**

**3.** Repeat step 2 with piles #3 and #5 to cut 20 (2½" x 10½") #3 units and 20 (2½" x 10½") #5 units.

**4.** Repeat step 2 with piles #2 and #4 to cut 20 (2½" x 10½") #2 units and 20 (2½" x 10½") #4 units, referring to Figure 2.

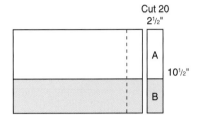

**Figure 2**

**5.** Referring to Figure 3, lay out one each of units #1–#5. Join the units together to make a block. Repeat to make 20 blocks.

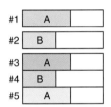

**Figure 3**

## Designer Tip

*The blocks in the second and fourth rows are arranged differently than in the top, middle and bottom rows. Be careful when assembling the top in order to get the building block look!*

## Completing the Quilt

Refer to the Assembly Diagram for positioning of blocks, rows and strips for steps 1–6.

**1.** Lay out the blocks into five rows of four blocks each. Sew the blocks into rows.

**2.** Join the rows to complete the quilt center; press.

**3.** Join C/D/G/H strips on the short ends to make a long strip; press. Subcut strip into two each 2" x 50½" C strips, 2" x 43½" D strips, 2" x 59½" G strips and 2" x 52½" H strips.

**4.** Sew C strips to opposite sides of the quilt center and D strips to the top and bottom, press.

**5.** Join E/F strips on the short ends to make a long strip; press. Subcut strip into two each 3½" x 53½" E strips and 3½" x 49½" F strips. Sew E strips to opposite sides of the quilt center and F strips to the top and bottom, press.

**6.** Sew G strips to opposite sides of the quilt center and H strips to the top and bottom to complete the quilt top, press.

**7.** Create a quilt sandwich referring to Quilting Basics on page 44.

**8.** Quilt as desired.

**9.** Bind referring to Quilting Basics on page 44 to finish. ●

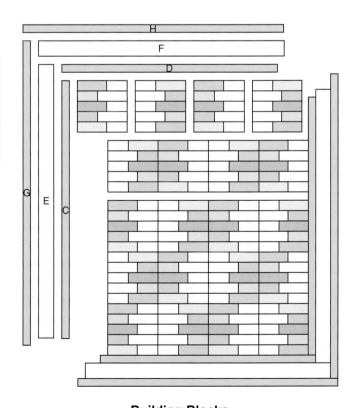

**Building Blocks**
Assembly Diagram 52" x 62"

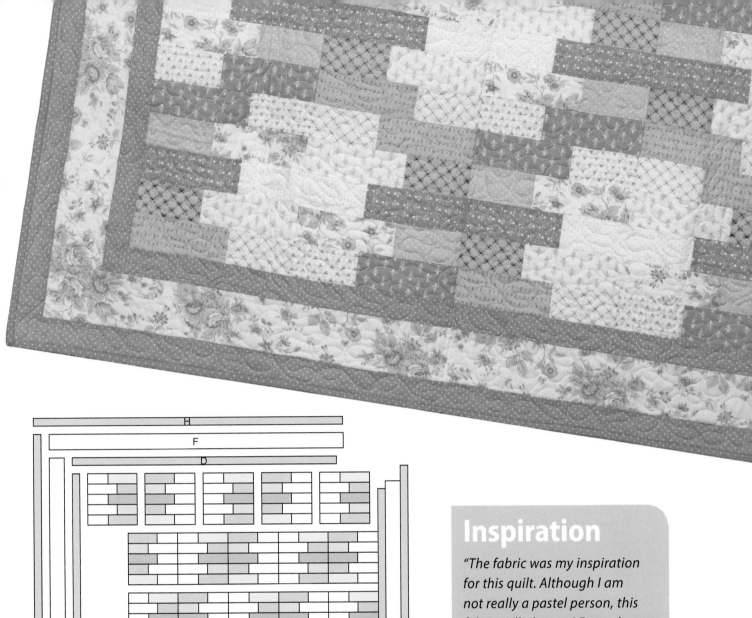

## Inspiration

*"The fabric was my inspiration for this quilt. Although I am not really a pastel person, this fabric called to me! Funny how fabric does that sometimes! The challenge for this book—designing quilts that could be made 'in a jiffy'—was also inspirational. I do like projects that go together quickly and look really nice. I'm so happy when a quilt like Building Blocks is the result!"* —Julie Weaver

**Building Blocks**
Alternate-Size Assembly Diagram 62" x 82"
Add 1 block to each row & 2 rows to
the length to make a twin-size quilt.

# Solitude

## This two-block wonder can easily be made in a day or two. Select your fabrics and get stitching.

### Designed & Quilted by Tricia Lynn Maloney

## Skill Level
Beginner

## Specifications
Quilt Size: 58" x 58"
Block Size: 10" x 10" finished
Number of Blocks: 25

## Materials
- ¼ yard aqua/yellow batik
- ½ yard teal/green batik
- ½ yard each green/orange batik
- ½ yard teal #1 batik
- ½ yard aqua batik
- ½ yard green batik
- 1 yard teal #2 batik
- 1⅝ yards dark blue/aqua batik
- Backing to size
- Batting to size
- Thread
- Basic sewing tools and supplies

## Project Notes
Read all instructions before beginning this project.

Stitch right sides together using a ¼" seam allowance unless otherwise specified.

Materials and cutting lists assume 40" of usable fabric width.

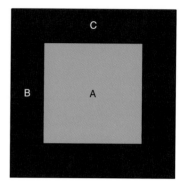

**Solitude**
10" x 10" Finished Block
Make 13

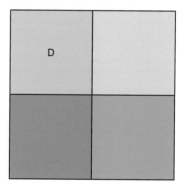

**Four-Patch**
10" x 10" Finished Block
Make 12

## Cutting

### From aqua/yellow batik:
- Cut 1 (6½" by fabric width) strip.
  Subcut strip into 6 (6½") A squares.

### From teal/green batik:
- Cut 2 (6½" by fabric width) strips.
  Subcut strips into 7 (6½") A squares.

## From each green/orange, teal #1, aqua & green batik:

- Cut 2 (5½" by fabric width) strips.
  Subcut strips into 12 (5½") D squares for a total of 48 D squares.

## From teal #2 batik:

- Cut 6 (4½" by fabric width) E/F strips.

## From dark blue/aqua batik:

- Cut 14 (2½" by fabric width) strips.
  Subcut strips into 26 (2½" x 6½") B rectangles and 26 (2½" x 10½") C rectangles.
- Cut 6 (2¼" by fabric width) strips for binding.

## Completing the Blocks

**1.** Referring to Figure 1a, sew a B rectangle to opposite sides of an A square. Sew a C rectangle to the top and bottom of A-B unit referring to Figure 1b. Repeat to make 13 Solitude blocks.

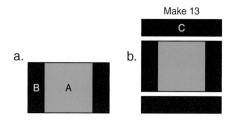

Make 13

**Figure 1**

**2.** Referring to Figure 2, sew four different D squares together to make a Four-Patch block. Repeat to make 12 Four-Patch blocks.

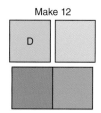

Make 12

**Figure 2**

## Completing the Quilt

Refer to the Assembly Diagram for positioning of blocks, rows and strips for steps 1–3.

**1.** Arrange and join the blocks into five rows of five blocks; press.

**2.** Join the rows to complete the quilt center; press.

**3.** Join the E/F strips on the short ends to make a long strip; press. Subcut strip into two 4½" x 50½" E strips and two 4½" x 58½" F strips. Sew E strips to opposite sides of the quilt center; press. Sew F strips to the top and bottom of the quilt center to complete the quilt top; press.

**4.** Create a quilt sandwich referring to Quilting Basics on page 44.

**5.** Quilt as desired.

**6.** Bind referring to Quilting Basics on page 44 to finish. ●

## Inspiration

*"Batik fabrics are so yummy— they really shine in simple quilt designs."* —Tricia Lynn Maloney

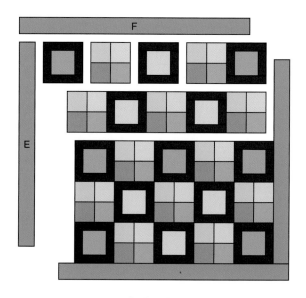

**Solitude**
Assembly Diagram 58" x 58"

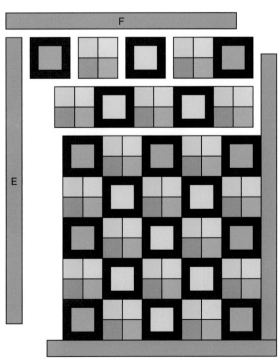

**Solitude**
Alternate-Size Assembly Diagram 58" x 78"
Add 2 rows to the length to make a twin-size quilt.

# Drifting

The combination of easy strip piecing and fusible appliqué are all that's needed to create this lovely quilt over a weekend.

Designed & Quilted by Carol Steely for FunThreads Designs, LLC

## Skill Level
Confident Beginner

## Specifications
Quilt Size: 48" x 55"
Block Size: 8" x 12" finished
Number of Blocks: 4

## Materials
- 2" x 4" black scrap
- ⅓ yard gold batik
- ½ yard orange batik
- ½ yard medium blue batik
- ½ yard light blue batik
- 1¼ yards white batik
- 1½ yards dark blue batik
- Backing to size
- Batting to size
- Thread
- ½ yard fusible web
- Template material
- Basic sewing tools and supplies

## Project Notes
Read all instructions before beginning this project.

Stitch right sides together using a ¼" seam allowance unless otherwise specified.

Materials and cutting lists assume 40" of usable fabric width.

**Sea Horse**
8" x 12" Finished Block
Make 4

## Cutting
Refer to Raw-Edge Appliqué sidebar on page 34 to prepare templates for the sea horse motif using pattern given on page 36; cut from the fabric as directed on pattern and in the instructions.

## Designer Tip
*Use a die-cutting machine for faster strip cutting.*

### From medium blue batik:
- Cut 4 (3½" by fabric width) strips.
  Subcut strips into 16 (3½" x 8½") B rectangles.

### From light blue batik:
- Cut 4 (3½" by fabric width) strips.
  Subcut strips into 16 (3½" x 8½") C rectangles.

### From white batik:

- Cut 4 (3½" by fabric width) E strips.
- Cut 5 (2½" by fabric width) F/G strips.
- Cut 1 (12½" by fabric width) strip.
  Subcut strip into 4 (8½" x 12½") D rectangles.

### From dark blue batik:

- Cut 4 (3½" by fabric width) strips.
  Subcut strips into 16 (3½" x 8½") A rectangles.
- Cut 6 (2" by fabric width) H/I strips.
- Cut 6 (2½" by fabric width) strips for binding.

## Designer Tip

*The full-size template is reversed and ready to use for fusible appliqué. If you trace the shape on the back of the sheet it can also be used as a placement guide under an appliqué pressing sheet.*

## Completing the Blocks

Refer to Raw-Edge Appliqué sidebar on page 34 for detailed instructions and to block drawing.

**1.** Referring to number to cut on pattern given, trace the shapes onto the paper side of the fusible web leaving ⅛"–¼" between pieces; cut out pieces leaving a margin around each one.

**2.** Fuse shapes to the wrong side of the indicated fabric; cut out shapes on traced lines. Remove paper backing.

**3.** Select one each top fin, back fin, body, eye, pupil and D rectangle to make one Sea Horse block. Fuse appliqué pieces to D in order noted on patterns. Repeat to make four blocks.

## Completing the Quilt

Refer to the Assembly Diagram for positioning of pieces, blocks, strips and rows for steps 1–4.

**1.** To make a vertical row, join two each A, B and C rectangles along length to make an upper unit. Repeat to make a lower unit. Sew the upper and lower units to the top and bottom of a Sea Horse block. In the same manner, make three more vertical rows, noting placement and number of A, B and C rectangles in upper and lower units, and placing units above and below blocks as shown.

**2.** Join the E strips on the short ends to make a long strip; press. Subcut strip into three 3½" x 48½" E sashing strips. Alternating placement, join the vertical rows and E sashing strips together.

**3.** Join the F/G strips on the short ends to make a long strip; press. Subcut strip into two 2½" x 48½" F strips and two 2½" x 45½" G strips. Sew F strips to opposite sides of the quilt center and G strips to the top and bottom; press.

**4.** Join the H/I strips on the short ends to make a long strip; press. Subcut strip into two 2" x 52½" H strips and two 2" x 48½" I strips. Sew H strips to opposite sides of the quilt center and I strips to the top and bottom to complete the quilt top; press.

**5.** Create a quilt sandwich referring to Quilting Basics on page 44.

**6.** Quilt as desired.

**7.** Bind referring to Quilting Basics on page 44 to finish. ●

## Inspiration

*"I love the way sea horses gently drift along. I grew up in south Jersey and have fun memories of summers in Wildwood and Atlantic City. Jersey Shore by Island Batik was a fitting collection to feature in this quilt."* —Carol Steely

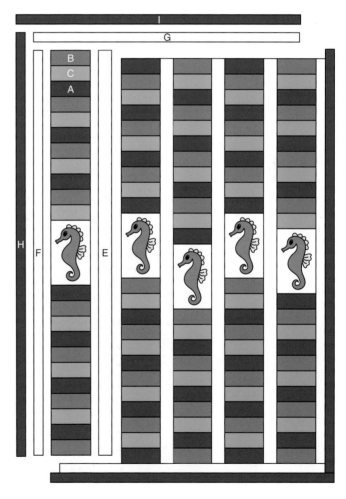

**Drifting**
Alternate-Size Assembly Diagram 59" x 85"
Add 5 blue rectangles to both top & bottom of each vertical row, & add 1 vertical row and 1 E sashing strip to make a twin-size quilt.

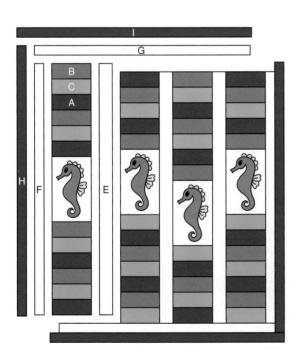

**Drifting**
Assembly Diagram 48" x 55"

# Raw-Edge Fusible Appliqué

One of the easiest ways to appliqué is the raw-edge fusible-web method. Paper-backed fusible web individual pieces are fused to the wrong side of specified fabrics, cut out and then fused together in a motif or individually to a foundation fabric, where they are machine-stitched in place.

## Choosing Appliqué Fabrics

Depending on the appliqué, you may want to consider using batiks. Batik is a much tighter weave and, because of the manufacturing process, does not fray. If you are thinking about using regular quilting cottons, be sure to stitch your raw-edge appliqués with blanket/buttonhole stitches instead of a straight stitch.

## Cutting Appliqué Pieces

**1.** Fusible appliqué shapes should be reversed for this technique.

**2.** Trace the appliqué shapes onto the paper side of paper-backed fusible web. Leave at least ¼" between shapes. Cut out shapes leaving a margin around traced lines. **Note:** *If doing several identical appliqués, trace reversed shapes onto template material to make reusable templates for tracing shapes onto the fusible web.*

**3.** Follow manufacturer's instructions and fuse shapes to wrong side of fabric as indicated on pattern for color and number to cut.

**4.** Cut out appliqué shapes on traced lines. Remove paper backing from shapes.

**5.** Again following fusible web manufacturer's instructions, arrange and fuse pieces to quilt referring to quilt pattern. Or fuse together shapes on top of an appliqué ironing mat to make an appliqué motif that can then be fused to the quilt.

## Stitching Appliqué Edges

Machine-stitch appliqué edges to secure the appliqués in place and help finish the raw edges with matching or invisible thread (Photo 1). **Note:** *To show stitching, all samples have been stitched with contrasting thread.*

Straight stitch

Buttonhole or blanket stitch

Photo 1

Invisible thread can be used to stitch appliqués down when using the blanket or straight stitches. Do not use it for the satin stitch. Definitely practice with invisible thread before using it on your quilt; it can sometimes be difficult to work with.

A short, narrow buttonhole or blanket stitch is most commonly used (Photo 2). Your machine manual may also refer to this as an appliqué stitch. Be sure to stitch next to the appliqué edge with the stitch catching the appliqué.

Photo 2

Practice turning inside and outside corners on scrap fabric before stitching appliqué pieces. Learn how your machine stitches so that you can make the pivot points smooth.

**1.** To stitch outer corners, stitch to the edge of the corner and stop with needle in the fabric at the corner point. Pivot to the next side of the corner and continue to sew (Photo 3). You will get a box on an outside corner.

Photo 3

**2.** To stitch inner corners, pivot at the inner point with needle in fabric (Photo 4). You will see a Y shape in the corner.

Photo 4

**3.** You can also use a machine straight stitch. Turn corners in the same manner, stitching to the corners and pivoting with needle in down position (Photo 5).

Photo 5

## General Appliqué Tips

**1.** Use a light- to medium-weight stabilizer behind an appliqué to keep the fabric from puckering during machine stitching (Photo 6).

Photo 6

**2.** To reduce the stiffness of a finished appliqué, cut out the center of the fusible web shape, leaving ¼"–½" inside the pattern line. This gives a border of adhesive to fuse to the background and leaves the center soft and easy to quilt.

**3.** If an appliqué fabric is so light colored or thin that the background fabric shows through, fuse a lightweight interfacing to the wrong side of the fabric. You can also fuse a piece of the appliqué fabric to a matching piece, wrong sides together, and then apply the fusible with a drawn pattern to one side.

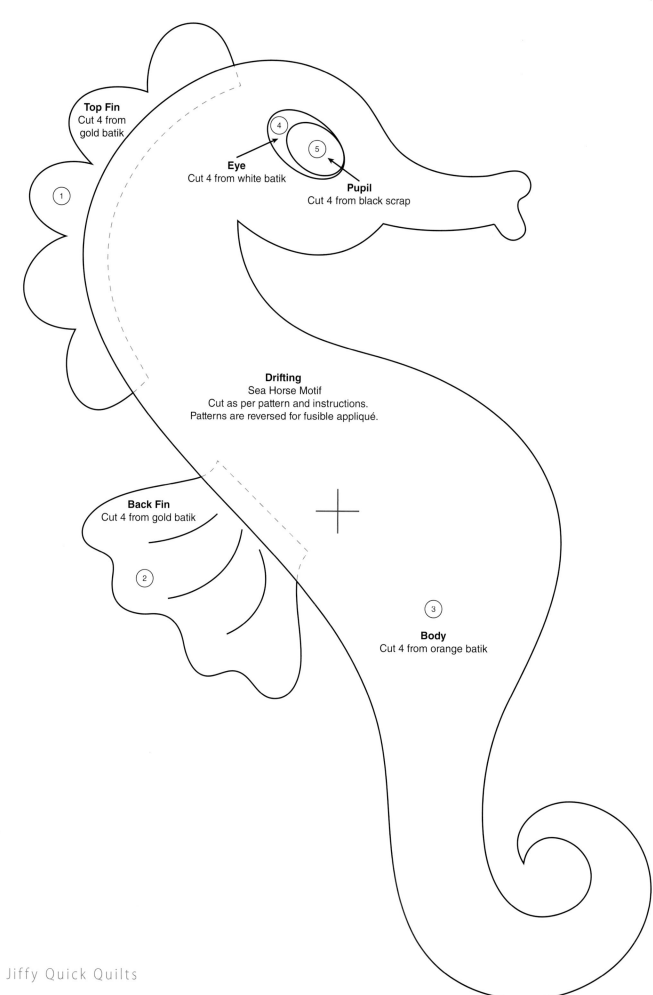

**Top Fin**
Cut 4 from
gold batik

1

**Eye**
Cut 4 from white batik

4

5

**Pupil**
Cut 4 from black scrap

**Drifting**
Sea Horse Motif
Cut as per pattern and instructions.
Patterns are reversed for fusible appliqué.

**Back Fin**
Cut 4 from gold batik

2

3

**Body**
Cut 4 from orange batik

# Sunday Brunch

Stitch up a watercolor garden for your table in an afternoon.

Designed & Quilted by Tricia Lynn Maloney

## Skill Level
Beginner

## Specifications
Runner Size: 54" x 18"

## Materials
- 44 assorted (5") precut squares
- ⅜ yard binding fabric
- ⅞ yard large floral
- Backing to size
- Batting to size
- Thread
- Basic sewing tools and supplies

## Project Notes
Read all instructions before beginning this project.

Stitch right sides together using a ¼" seam allowance unless otherwise specified.

Materials and cutting lists assume 40" of usable fabric width.

## Cutting

### From assorted 5" precut squares:
- Trim each square to make a 3½" B square.

### From binding fabric:
- Cut 4 (2¼" by fabric width) strips for binding.

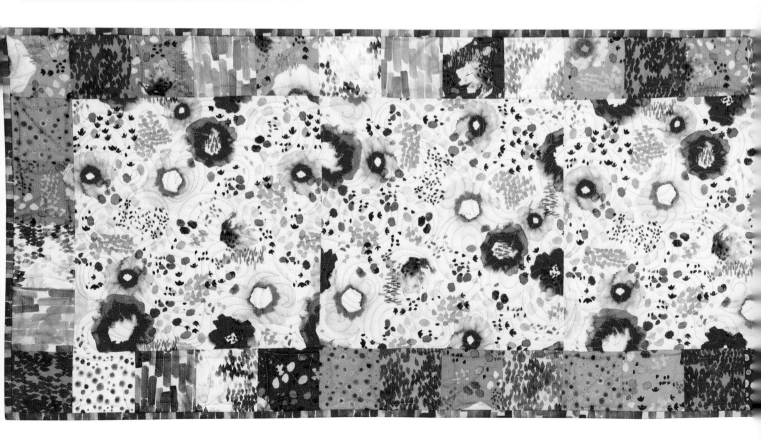

## From large floral:
- Cut 2 (12½" by fabric width) strips.
  Subcut strips into 4 (12½") A squares.

## Completing the Runner

Refer to the Assembly Diagram for positioning of pieces for steps 2 and 3.

**1.** Sew the four A squares together as shown in Figure 1.

**Figure 1**

**2.** Sew 16 B squares together to make a long border. Repeat to make a second long border. Sew long borders to the long edges of the A unit.

**3.** Sew six B squares together to make a short border. Repeat to make a second short border. Sew short borders to the short edges of the A unit.

**4.** Create a quilt sandwich referring to Quilting Basics on page 44.

**5.** Quilt as desired.

**6.** Bind referring to Quilting Basics on page 44 to finish. ●

## Inspiration

*"Simple quilts have a beauty and charm all of their own. Add amazing fabrics to a simple design to make it extraordinary!"* —Tricia Lynn Maloney

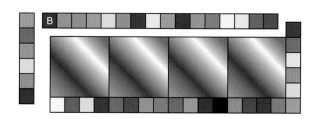

**Sunday Brunch**
Assembly Diagram 54" x 18"

# Gentle Breeze

A simple block pattern and a fun collection of fabrics
are all you need to stitch up a gorgeous quilt.

Design by Bev Getschel
Quilted by Lynette Gelling

## Skill Level
Beginner

## Specifications
Quilt Size: 76" x 92"
Block Size: 8" x 8" finished
Number of Blocks: 70

## Materials
- ⅔ yard each 10 assorted prints
- 1½ yards gray solid
- 2½ yards aqua border stripe
- Backing to size
- Batting to size
- Thread
- Basic sewing tools and supplies

## Project Notes
Read all instructions before beginning this project.

Stitch right sides together using a ¼" seam
allowance unless otherwise specified.

Materials and cutting lists assume 40" of usable
fabric width.

## Cutting

### From 10 assorted prints:
- Cut 2 (9½" by fabric width) strips from each print.
  Subcut strips into 70 (9½") A squares.

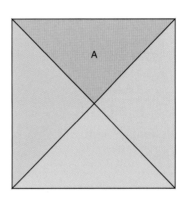

**Hourglass**
8" x 8" Finished Block
Make 70

### From gray solid:
- Cut 3 (8½" by fabric width) strips.
  Subcut strips into 10 (8½") B squares.
- Cut 9 (2¼" by fabric width) strips for binding.

### From aqua border stripe:
- Cut 2 (6½" x 80½") lengthwise C strips,
  centering motif.
- Cut 2 (6½" x 76½") lengthwise D strips,
  centering motif.

## Completing the Blocks

**1.** Draw a diagonal line from corner to corner on the
wrong side of 35 A squares.

**2.** Referring to Figure 1, place a marked A square
right sides together on an unmarked A square. Stitch
¼" on both sides of the drawn line; cut on drawn line.
Press both units open. Repeat to make 70 A units.

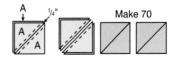

**Figure 1**

**3.** Draw a diagonal line from corner to corner across the seam on the wrong side of 35 A units.

**4.** Referring to Figure 2, place a marked A unit right sides together on an unmarked A unit matching seams. Stitch ¼" on both sides of the drawn line; cut on drawn line. Press both blocks open. Trim blocks to measure 8½" square, centering seam in square. Repeat to make 70 Hourglass blocks.

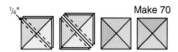

**Figure 2**

## Completing the Quilt

Refer to the Assembly Diagram for positioning of pieces for steps 1–3.

**1.** Lay out the Hourglass blocks and 10 B squares into 10 rows of 8 blocks and squares each. Sew the blocks and squares into rows.

**2.** Join the rows to complete the quilt center; press.

**3.** Sew C strips to opposite sides, and D strips to the top and bottom of the quilt center to complete the quilt top; press.

**4.** Create a quilt sandwich referring to Quilting Basics on page 44.

**5.** Quilt as desired.

**6.** Bind referring to Quilting Basics on page 44 to finish. ●

## Inspiration

*"I was thinking about fast and easy and started the design process with 10" squares in mind. When I saw this soft as a whisper collection it spoke to me."* —Bev Getschel

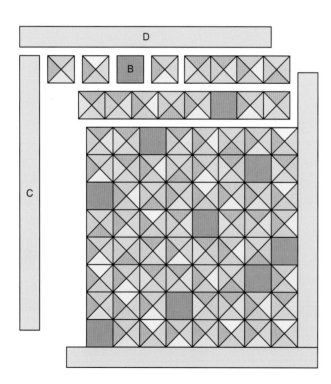

**Gentle Breeze**
Assembly Diagram 76" x 92"

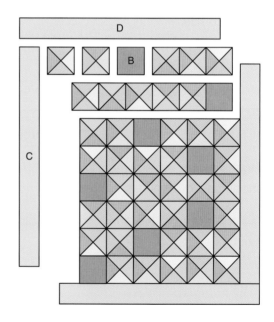

**Gentle Breeze**
Alternate-Size Assembly Diagram 60" x 76"
Remove 2 blocks from each row & 2 rows from the length to make a lap-size quilt.

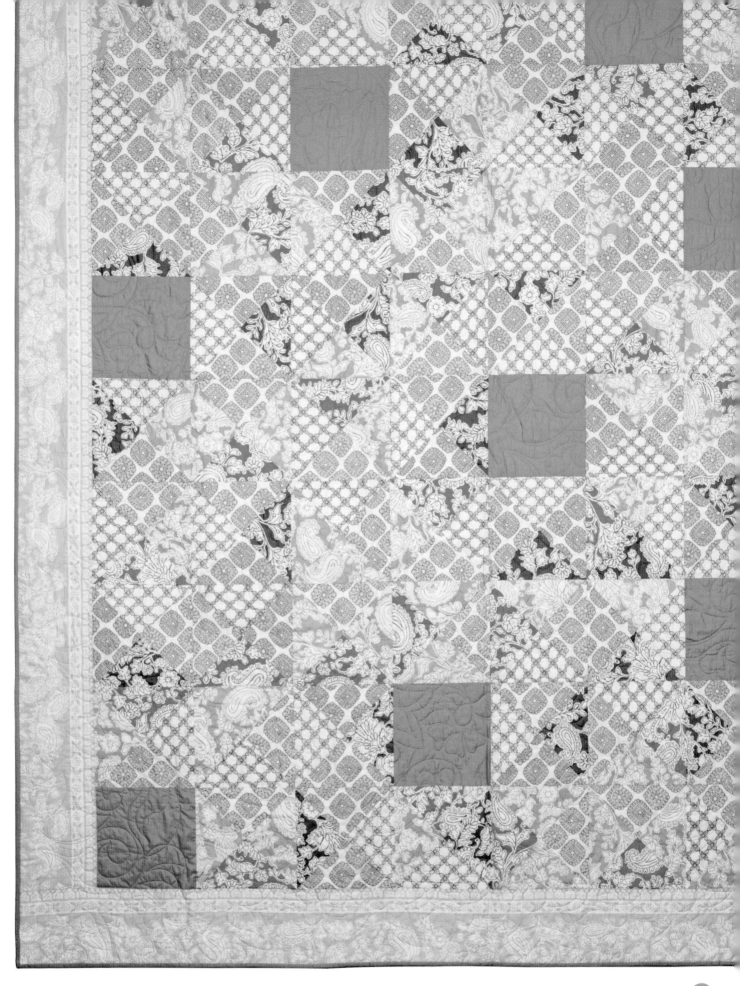

# Quilting Basics

The following is a reference guide. For more information, consult a comprehensive quilting book.

## Always:

- Read through the entire pattern before you begin your project.
- Purchase quality, 100 percent cotton fabrics.
- When considering prewashing, do so with ALL of the fabrics being used. Generally, prewashing is not required in quilting.
- Use ¼" seam allowance for all stitching unless otherwise instructed.
- Use a short-to-medium stitch length.
- Make sure your seams are accurate.

## Quilting Tools & Supplies

- Rotary cutter and mat
- Scissors for paper and fabric
- Non-slip quilting rulers
- Marking tools
- Sewing machine
- Sewing machine feet:
    ¼" seaming foot (for piecing)
    Walking or even-feed foot
      (for piecing or quilting)
    Darning or free-motion foot
      (for free-motion quilting)
- Quilting hand-sewing needles
- Straight pins
- Curved safety pins for basting
- Seam ripper
- Iron and ironing surface

## Basic Techniques

### Appliqué

**Fusible Appliqué**

All templates are reversed for use with this technique.

**1.** Trace the instructed number of templates ¼" apart onto the paper side of paper-backed fusible web. Cut apart the templates, leaving a margin around each, and fuse to the wrong side of the fabric following fusible web manufacturer's instructions.

**2.** Cut the appliqué pieces out on the traced lines, remove paper backing and fuse to the background referring to the appliqué motif given.

**3.** Finish appliqué raw edges with a straight, satin, blanket, zigzag or blind-hem machine stitch with matching or invisible thread.

### Turned-Edge Appliqué

**1.** Trace the printed reversed templates onto template plastic. Flip the template over and mark as the right side.

**2.** Position the template, right side up, on the right side of fabric and lightly trace, spacing images ½" apart. Cut apart, leaving a ¼" margin around the traced lines.

**3.** Clip curves and press edges ¼" to the wrong side around the appliqué shape.

**4.** Referring to the appliqué motif, pin or baste appliqué shapes to the background.

**5.** Hand-stitch shapes in place using a blind stitch and thread to match or machine-stitch using a short blind hemstitch and either matching or invisible thread.

### Borders

Most patterns give an exact size to cut borders. You may check those sizes by comparing them to the horizontal and vertical center measurements of your quilt top.

### Straight Borders

**1.** Mark the centers of the side borders and quilt top sides.

**2.** Stitch borders to quilt top sides with right sides together and matching raw edges and center marks using a ¼" seam. Press seams toward borders.

**3.** Repeat with top and bottom border lengths.

### Mitered Borders

**1.** Add at least twice the border width to the border lengths instructed to cut.

**2.** Center and sew the side borders to the quilt, beginning and ending stitching ¼" from the quilt corner and backstitching (Figure 1). Repeat with the top and bottom borders.

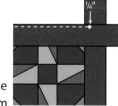

**Figure 1**

**3.** Fold and pin quilt right sides together at a 45-degree angle on one corner (Figure 2). Place a straightedge along the fold and lightly mark a line across the border ends.

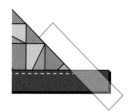

**Figure 2**

**4.** Stitch along the line, backstitching to secure. Trim seam to ¼" and press open (Figure 3).

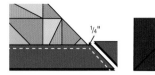

**Figure 3**

### Quilt Backing & Batting

We suggest that you cut your backing and batting 8" larger than the finished quilt-top size. If preparing the backing from standard-width fabrics, remove the selvages and sew two or three lengths together; press seams open. If using 108"-wide fabric, trim to size on the straight grain of the fabric.

Prepare batting the same size as your backing. You can purchase prepackaged sizes or battings by the yard and trim to size.

### Quilting

**1.** Press quilt top on both sides and trim all loose threads.

**2.** Make a quilt sandwich by layering the backing right side down, batting and quilt top centered right side up on flat surface and smooth out. Pin or baste layers together to hold.

**3.** Mark quilting design on quilt top and quilt as desired by hand or machine. *Note: If you are sending your quilt to a professional quilter, contact them for specifics about preparing your quilt for quilting.*

**4.** When quilting is complete, remove pins or basting. Trim batting and backing edges even with raw edges of quilt top.

### Binding the Quilt

**1.** Join binding strips on short ends with diagonal seams to make one long strip; trim seams to ¼" and press seams open (Figure 4).

**2.** Fold 1" of one short end to wrong side and press. Fold the binding strip in half with wrong sides together along length, again referring to Figure 4; press.

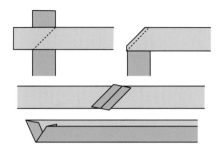

**Figure 4**

**3.** Starting about 3" from the folded short end, sew binding to quilt top edges, matching raw edges and using a ¼" seam. Stop stitching ¼" from corner and backstitch (Figure 5).

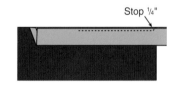

Stop ¼"

**Figure 5**

**4.** Fold binding up at a 45-degree angle to seam and then down even with quilt edges, forming a pleat at corner, referring to Figure 6.

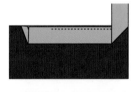

**Figure 6**

**5.** Resume stitching from corner edge as shown in Figure 6, down quilt side, backstitching ¼" from next corner. Repeat, mitering all corners, stitching to within 3" of starting point.

**6.** Trim binding end long enough to tuck inside starting end and complete stitching (Figure 7).

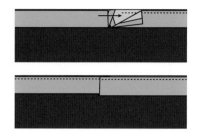

**Figure 7**

**7.** Fold binding to quilt back and stitch in place by hand or machine to complete your quilt.

## Quilting Terms

- **Appliqué:** Adding fabric motifs to a foundation fabric by hand or machine (see Appliqué section of Basic Techniques).

- **Basting:** This temporarily secures layers of quilting materials together with safety pins, thread or a spray adhesive in preparation for quilting the layers.

  Use a long, straight stitch to hand- or machine-stitch one element to another holding the elements in place during construction and usually removed after construction.

- **Batting:** An insulating material made in a variety of fiber contents that is used between the quilt top and back to provide extra warmth and loft.

- **Binding:** A finishing strip of fabric sewn to the outer raw edges of a quilt to cover them.

  Straight-grain binding strips, cut on the crosswise straight grain of the fabric (see Straight & Bias Grain Lines illustration on page 46), are commonly used.

  Bias binding strips are cut at a 45-degree angle to the straight grain of the fabric. They are used when binding is being added to curved edges.

- **Block:** The basic quilting unit that is repeated to complete the quilt's design composition. Blocks can be pieced, appliquéd or solid and are usually square or rectangular in shape.
- **Border:** The frame of a quilt's central design used to visually complete the design and give the eye a place to rest.
- **Fabric Grain:** The fibers that run either parallel (lengthwise grain) or perpendicular (crosswise grain) to the fabric selvage are straight grain.

  Bias is any diagonal line between the lengthwise or crosswise grain. At these angles the fabric is less stable and stretches easily. The true bias of a woven fabric is a 45-degree angle between the lengthwise and crosswise grain lines.

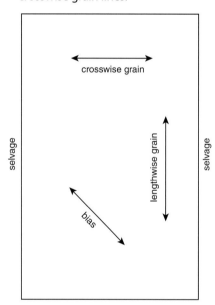

**Straight & Bias Grain Lines**

- **Mitered Corners:** Matching borders or turning bindings at a 45-degree angle at corners.
- **Patchwork:** A general term for the completed blocks or quilts that are made from smaller shapes sewn together.

- **Pattern:** This may refer to the design of a fabric or to the written instructions for a particular quilt design.
- **Piecing:** The act of sewing smaller pieces and/or units of a block or quilt together.

  Paper or foundation piecing is sewing fabric to a paper or cloth foundation in a certain order.

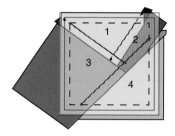

**Foundation Piecing**

String or chain piecing is sewing pieces together in a continuous string without clipping threads between sections.

**String or Chain Piecing**

- **Pressing:** Pressing is the process of placing the iron on the fabric, lifting it off the fabric and placing it down in another location to flatten seams or crease fabric without sliding the iron across the fabric.

  Quilters do not usually use steam when pressing, since it can easily distort fabric shapes.

  Generally, seam allowances are pressed toward the darker fabric in quilting so that they do not show through the lighter fabric.

  Seams are pressed in opposite directions where seams are being joined to allow seams to butt against each other and to distribute bulk.

Seams are pressed open when multiple seams come together in one place.

If you have a question about pressing direction, consult a comprehensive quilting guide for guidance.

- **Quilt (noun):** A sandwich of two layers of fabric with a third insulating material between them that is then stitched together with the edges covered or bound.
- **Quilt (verb):** Stitching several layers of fabric materials together with a decorative design. Stippling, cross-hatch, channel, in-the-ditch, free-motion, allover and meandering are all terms for quilting designs.

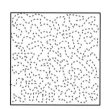

**Meandering**

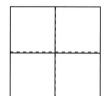

**Stitch-in-the-ditch**

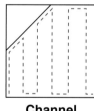

**Channel**

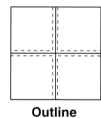

**Outline**

- **Quilt Sandwich:** The layering of the quilt's backing fabric, batting, and quilt top.
- **Rotary Cutting:** Using a rotary cutting blade and straightedge to cut fabric.
- **Sashing:** Strips of fabric sewn between blocks to separate or set off the designs.
- **Subcut:** A second cutting of rotary-cut strips that makes the basic shapes used in block and quilt construction.
- **Template:** A pattern made from a sturdy material which is then used to cut shapes for patchwork and appliqué quilting.

## Quilting Skill Levels

- **Beginner:** A quilter who has been introduced to the basics of cutting, piecing and assembling a quilt top and is working to master these skills. Someone who has the knowledge of how to sandwich, quilt and bind a quilt, but may not have necessarily accomplished the task yet.

- **Confident Beginner:** A quilter who has pieced and assembled several quilt tops and is comfortable with the process, and is now ready to move on to more challenging techniques and projects using at least two different techniques.

- **Intermediate:** A quilter who is comfortable with most quilting techniques and has a good understanding for design, color and the whole process. A quilter who is experienced in paper piecing, bias piecing and projects involving multiple techniques. Someone who is confident in making fabric selections other than those listed in the pattern.

- **Advanced:** A quilter who is looking for a challenging design. Someone who knows she or he can make any type of quilt. Someone who has the skills to read, comprehend and complete a pattern, and is willing to take on any technique. A quilter who is comfortable in her or his skills and has the ability to select fabric suited to the project. ●

# Special Thanks

Please join us in thanking the talented designers
whose work is featured in this collection.

**Gina Gempesaw**
Fly Right, page 8
Twist It & Turn It, page 17

**Bev Getschel**
Gentle Breeze, page 41

**Tricia Lynn Maloney**
Solitude, page 26
Sunday Brunch, page 37

**Denise Russell**
Lemonade, page 5

**Nancy Scott**
Cake Walk, page 2

**Carol Steely**
Drifting, page 30

**Julie Weaver**
Building Blocks, page 23
Tiny Bubbles, page 12

# Supplies

We would like to thank the following manufacturers who
provided materials to make sample projects for this book.

**Cake Walk, page 2:** Chromatics collection from Art Gallery Fabrics.

**Lemonade, page 5:** Simply Colorful, Essential Dots, Marbles and Bella fabrics from Moda Fabrics.

**Tiny Bubbles, page 12:** Hi-De-Ho and Bella Solids fabric from Moda Fabrics; Thermore Ultra Thin Polyester Batting from Hobbs Bonded Fibers.

**Building Blocks, page 23:** Kindred Spirits fabric from Moda Fabrics; Thermore Ultra Thin Polyester Batting from Hobbs Bonded Fibers.

**Solitude, page 26:** Batik Paradise and Birchtree Lane Fabrics, Essential thread and Hobbs Heirloom Premium 80/20 batting, all from Connecting Threads.

**Drifting, page 30:** Jersey Shore and Milkshake fabrics from Island Batik.

**Sunday Brunch, page 37:** Flora collection from Windham Fabrics; Quilter's 80/20 Batting from Fairfield.

**Gentle Breeze, page 41:** Whisper collection from Michael Miller Fabrics; American Spirit Batting from Fairfield.

*Annie's* ® *Jiffy Quick Quilts* is published by Annie's, 306 East Parr Road, Berne, IN 46711. Printed in USA. Copyright © 2015, 2017 Annie's. All rights reserved. This publication may not be reproduced in part or in whole without written permission from the publisher.

**RETAIL STORES:** If you would like to carry this publication or any other Annie's publications, visit AnniesWSL.com.

Every effort has been made to ensure that the instructions in this publication are complete and accurate. We cannot, however, take responsibility for human error, typographical mistakes or variations in individual work. Please visit AnniesCustomerService.com to check for pattern updates.

ISBN: 978-1-57367-963-3

10